24 talk ideas for all-age services

kevin mayhew

Published in 2006 by

KEVIN MAYHEW LTD
Buxhall, Stowmarket, Suffolk, IP14 3BW
E-mail: info@kevinmayhewltd.com
www.kevinmayhew.com

9 8 7 6 5 4 3 2 1 0

ISBN 1 84417 555 3
Catalogue No. 1500904

Cover design by Sara-Jane Came
Edited by Phil Green
Typesetting by Richard Weaver

Printed and bound in Great Britain

Contents

FS – Family Service
B – Baptism

Introduction

Many churches now have Baptism in a main service; and many churches have a regular 'Family' or non-Eucharistic service (at one church where I was the minister we called it 'Prayer and Praise'). These two different services share one characteristic – they are often attended by those who are not regular churchgoers.

My response to this experience was to use a different style of sermon (or talk as it soon became called). I found myself using visual aids and a simpler style in the hope that some of the message might stick. I tended not to rate these as highly as 'proper' sermons until one day a churchwarden said to me, 'I really like your Baptism talks. I can understand them.'

I now think this style is as valid in its setting as the more traditional sermon. These talks tend to be shorter (5 to 7 minutes) but they are still intended to say something important, and to teach. I offer them in the hope that you may find them useful, and with thanks to David who convinced me that this way would also serve the cause of the gospel.

How to use this book

There is a Baptism talk and a Family Service talk for each month of the year, though most of them could be used in any month. Where there is either a linked or an appropriate Bible reading I have shown this, but most of them stand alone.

I would not recommend that you read them out or deliver them exactly as set out. I can never use anyone else's sermons so I see no reason why it should be different for anyone else. The theme and the approach are here and I suggest you put the talk into your own words. Sometimes an example given is personal to me, but I am sure there will be similar examples you can use from your experience. My intention is to give you some ideas from which to start.

I think the method of delivery will need to vary according to the congregation. There will be some with whom you can engage in 'Question and Answer' ('What have I got here?' becomes a real question and you engage with them) and others who will not cope with this at all. You will have to judge which method suits your congregation best.

All of these have been used at Family or Baptism Services.

THE STAR

Bible Reading: Matthew 2:1-12

Prop A star (preferably large) from a Christmas tree.

Message Christmas is over but we can learn from the Wise Men.

Talk What have I got here? Yes – it is a star, from the Christmas tree. Epiphany marks that moment at which we pack away the Christmas decorations, and for many people that's also the signal to forget about Jesus for another year. The star, however, tells us otherwise. It reminds us of the Wise Men.

Vicars, like me, can be very dull about the Wise Men. We point out every year that they are NOT kings, and that the Bible never says there are three of them – it is three gifts, or even more boringly three sorts of gift. We then usually end our talk by inviting everyone to sing 'We Three Kings'.

Why we do this I am not quite sure, as I doubt anyone is listening. The pity of it is that the Wise Men are important as they can teach us such a lot about Jesus. There may not be three kings but there are, at least, three lessons we can learn from the Wise Men. They took time and trouble to find Jesus, they recognised him when they found him and offered him the best they could, and then, after meeting Jesus they had to return home, to normal life.

I think it is fair to assume that it wasn't an easy journey. It involved time, and trouble, and expense, and I expect their friends and families thought they were quite mad. We are lucky in that we know about Jesus but we often behave as if we want it all to be easy and without any difficulty for us. If you really want to find Jesus you have to make a real effort. It may involve things that are unfamiliar, like reading the Bible, saying your prayers, and coming to church – but how difficult are these things compared to what the Wise Men did?

The Wise Men succeeded in their task. They found Jesus, the baby they were looking for. When they did that they did not say how clever THEY had been but they offered this small child presents. Over the years Christians have seen lots of symbolism in the Wise Men's gifts, and this may be right. What is clear is that these presents were expensive and special, and that says to me that they were giving Jesus the very best they had. Christians are asked to be generous with their resources, but they are also asked to offer to Jesus the very best that they have, the best of themselves.

And then they went home. I wonder what it felt like when the excitement of the journey, the discovery of the child, and the giving of the presents, was all over? It must have felt odd and yet I cannot imagine that they were ever the same again; I doubt that they forgot about Jesus when they returned to ordinary life. They had encountered Jesus and they would carry that with them as long as they lived. That is true for every Christian. It is lovely to meet Jesus at special times of the year and Christmas is particularly fun both at home and in church, but Christmas finishes – and yet a person, having met Jesus, is never the same again.

You can put this star away in a box until next year, but don't do the same with Jesus. It takes trouble to find him, but it is worth it. He demands the best of what we are, but it is worth it. He doesn't disappear along with the Christmas decorations; he is always with us, even in everyday, ordinary life.

The star may come off the tree. But the lessons it teaches us are with us every day.

THE TRAIN TICKET

Prop A train ticket (or a bus/coach/air ticket). A passport can be used with only slight amendment.

Message Baptism is a good start, but you have to do something with it.

Talk What have I got here? A train ticket. I recently had to go to London so I bought a ticket. This one.

So was that it? I'd bought my ticket so was I already in London?

(With the right congregation, especially one with children I might do this as a question and answer but you can just carry on.) No, of course not. There was still something essential I had to do. I HAD TO GET ON THE TRAIN. All the ticket did was to allow me to travel. If I wanted to go anywhere I still had to get on the train.

All of which must seem very obvious to you. It is odd, then, that so many people get it wrong with Baptism. They seem to think that Baptism (or Christening) is both ticket and journey. They are wrong.

Baptism is important, it is the beginning of a journey. The 'ticket' of Baptism is for the journey of faith and it never runs out. Sadly, many people seem to forget that Baptism is the ticket, not the journey or destination. Baptism is a great start to life; how sad it is then that so many parents take no further action. They do nothing to help their child learn more about Christianity, to read the Bible, to pray, or to meet with other Christians in worship. They seem to think they have done everything that is needed.

They are wrong. Life is a journey. Baptism is a great ticket to have, but you still have to USE the ticket if you are going to get anywhere.

Make sure *this child/these children* don't get left behind. Help them aboard the train of faith.

THE BLOW, THE MONEY – AND THE THEFT!

Bible Reading: Matthew 5:38-48; Luke 6:27-38

Prop None – see beginning of talk.

Message We are called to live beyond the rule book.

Talk *(The talk begins with me going into the congregation – it is often better if this has been set up beforehand, but not essential. First, I strike a blow, very gently, on someone. Then I get someone to lend me some money. Finally, I take something off someone, for example, an umbrella.)*

Thank you all. You will understand, of course, that the person I hit must turn the other cheek – so I will be back in a moment to hit them again. The one I borrowed the money from must not expect it back. And, well, it is a nice umbrella – and I think I will keep it. What's the problem with any of that? After all, I am only asking you to behave as it said in the Gospel readings this morning. Turn the other cheek, and so on.

You are hoping I am not serious. But it is what Jesus says. And ever since he said it Christians have been trying to wrestle with how to live normal lives and live up to this seemingly impossible standard. Usually they have concluded that it can't be done – that it is an ideal that would be lovely to achieve but somehow real life doesn't allow it.

That is not very satisfactory, is it? So let us look again at where this passage of Scripture comes in our Bible. In St Matthew it is a part of the Sermon on the Mount. In Luke it is in the equivalent, if less well known, Sermon on the Plain. This is a block of teaching setting out NOT a new set of rules – the Jewish people had enough of those already – but, I suggest, a standard as to the sort of people we ought to be. The Sermon on the Mount in Matthew begins with the Beatitudes, a list of people who are 'blessed', not through deeds but because of what they are like AS PEOPLE. Jesus is, I think, trying to move us away from our usual desire for a clear list of rules to follow, where we believe that if we do follow them then we will be all right. He is asking us not to stay out of trouble by obeying the rules, but to be the kind of people God wants us to be and made us capable of being. The usual human response is to deal with people according to the rules and give them what they deserve. If we are wronged we want revenge. If we give we expect to receive in return.

God is not like that. God loves us and cares for us even when we do not deserve it. Jesus asks us to respond by living that out too. We are asked to make more effort than seems necessary or fair. We are asked to be ready to give and not get something back. We are encouraged to be loving and giving, even when the person you love or give to lets you down.

We are asked to live BEYOND THE RULE BOOK. We are called upon to do far more than is reasonable, even to an unreasonable extent. We are even to deliberately allow it not to be fair, and for us to be on the wrong side of that. It is very hard and yet, when one tries it, even a little, a most extraordinary thing happens: the world around is transformed. Generosity and love don't appear to pay off, and then suddenly everything is better when they are shown. It doesn't make sense. Not our sense anyway, but it seems instead to make God's sense.

God's sense – to live beyond the rule book.

FOLLOW ME!

Bible Reading: Matthew 4:18-22; Mark 1:16-20

Prop Members of the congregation (you will see!).

Message We can follow Jesus because he can be trusted.

Talk I wonder if you would do something for me? Would you mind getting up and following me? *(This might be to all the children present, the Junior Choir, those on one side of the church, or the whole congregation. It needs to be a significant number. I then say 'Follow me' and proceed round the church, according to my whim. Up and down and round about will do nicely. Finally, I let everyone sit down.)*

Why did you follow me? It was very nice that you did, but why? I suppose the real answer is that you trusted me not to do anything too unpleasant to you. You trusted me, and you were right to do so.

But then you know me, and I was not asking very much of you. Jesus asked his first disciples to make a complete change of life when he said 'Follow me' which is what our Gospel today is all about. 'Follow me' was not just a short walk around a familiar building. It was a 'nothing will ever be the same again' moment. We are not told if these first disciples had ever met Jesus before – I have certainly heard it suggested that they had seen Jesus before and knew him, but we can't say either one way or the other. Whether this had started long before or not, Jesus said, 'Follow me' – in everything. They did, and they can only have done that if, for whatever reason, they trusted Jesus completely. They cannot have imagined what it would mean in practice, but they still obeyed.

Jesus makes the same demand on every follower that he made on those four fishermen. 'Follow me,' he says. He doesn't tell us where we are going, but he asks us to come and follow him. We can know quite a lot about him as we have the Gospels and the life of the church over two thousand years to help us. But at the end of the day it still amounts to a matter of trust. Do we trust him enough to answer his call? Today we baptise *this child/these children* and as they grow and develop in their faith they will all be asked the same question by Jesus, 'Will you follow me?' It's a question we must answer for ourselves and help our children in due time to answer it too.

'Follow me,' says Jesus. 'Will you follow me?' You trusted me enough to follow me round this church. Jesus is much more worth following – for the whole of your lives.

You can follow me if you want to, but it's far more important, and far better to follow Jesus.

FORGIVE US OUR TRESPASSES

Prop Two people (arranged beforehand).

Message Forgiveness may be hard but it is essential.

Talk *(As the speaker takes his/her place two people come forward, squabbling as they do. 'It is all your fault.' 'No it isn't.' 'How could you do that?' 'I've done nothing.' 'I will never forgive you.' The speaker tries to get them to shake hands and 'forgive and forget'. They shake their heads instead, and stand with their backs to each other. Ideally they stay there throughout the talk.)*

What have we got here? Two people, cross with each other. It is not exactly new, is it? It happens all the time, to everyone, however young or old you are. Nearly every one of us has someone with whom we have fallen out at some time. And yet, if we are Christians, we probably use the Lord's Prayer and pray, 'Forgive us our trespasses – as we forgive those who trespass against us.'

It is a good thing that God is so much quicker to forgive us, than we often are to forgive other people. It is a good thing God doesn't have the attitude most of us have of 'I am not going to apologise – it was their fault.' God loves us, shambles though we sometimes are. God forgives us all the time. At nearly every service we have a Confession, where we recognise that we fall short of what we ought to be, and ask God to let us begin again.

There was a new, youngish minister, who visited a lady, in a village, whom he had previously seen in hospital. As he stood in the kitchen waiting for a cup of tea to be made he suddenly said, 'You must back on to Mrs so-and-so. She is such a nice lady. Do you know her well?' 'We don't speak,' came the reply. 'Dear me,' he said. 'Why ever not – you are both so pleasant.' 'We don't speak,' came the reply again. 'Our mothers didn't speak and we don't either.' *(And I should know because the minister was me!)*

What a shame, and what a waste! We could all tell such stories. Clergy well tell you of people at funerals sobbing because they never made up a quarrel and now it can never be mended. Friends fall out over something that years later neither of them can remember. Children leave home and never ring to say they are OK, and then find it harder and harder to ring when their parents just long to know they are well and happy. Again I say, what a shame and what a waste!

People give up things for Lent and that may be a good thing to do, not to let any desire take hold of us. I suggest it is better to do something positive, to make life better than it was before and do something which will last. I therefore ask everyone here who has fallen out with someone to go out and make the first move. Don't worry about whose fault the break-up was. Try not to re-ignite the quarrel. Make an approach and offer friendship. You may be rebuffed. If so, I am sorry, but in many cases the other person has been longing to end the division and has not known how to.

Forgive us our trespasses, as we forgive those who trespass against us.

(Turn to the pair. 'For goodness sake you two, you ought to be friends. Shake hands and be done with it, whoever's fault it was.' And they do just that.)

THE CROSS

Prop The cross.

Message Nothing is going to happen to us that Jesus hasn't experienced.

Talk What have I got here? *(produce a cross or crucifix)*, and here? *(points to a cross)*, and here? *(points again)*. Crosses everywhere, because it IS the symbol of the Christian faith. The sign of the cross is used in the Baptism here this morning, a reminder that the Christian faith goes back to Jesus, the man on the cross.

You might think that it is an odd symbol to use, as it represents a particularly horrible and unpleasant death, a bit like using a gallows or an electric chair. It is one of the significant things about Christianity that it is prepared to trace its origins back to a man who, in human terms, was a failure, executed by the authorities of his day with minimal protests on his behalf. Christians believe that the failure was apparent rather than real because we believe that Jesus was raised again on the first Easter Day. Easter is with us soon and one of the themes of Holy Week is that Palm Sunday looks like a triumph but is ultimately a disaster, whereas Good Friday looks like a disaster but is ultimately a triumph.

There is more than that, though. The cross tells us that God cared so much about this world that he came into it, and was prepared to endure the very worst that could happen. This means that whatever terrible things may happen in our lives, we can always turn to Jesus to be with us and sustain us. The cross reminds us that nothing can ever happen to us that Jesus hasn't experienced.

Teach these children that the cross is not just a convenient symbol, nor is it a nice piece of jewellery to wear. It is a declaration that the man on the cross is the one we follow and he can go anywhere with us because he has already been there.

(This is one of the shorter talks at Baptism. I think this makes it more effective. It is not 'fun' like some of them, but it is not complicated either.)

FOOTWASHING

Bible Reading: John 13:1-15

Prop A bowl, a flannel and a towel. Possibly volunteers.

(This will depend on circumstances, such as the date of Easter in a year, and whether a church has a foot-washing ceremony on Maundy Thursday. This talk could be used at a different time of the year and reference made to Maundy Thursday. I have assumed this will be a talk at a Family Service in April not in Holy Week or on Easter Day.)

Message No service is 'beneath us'.

Talk What have I got here? Look – a bowl, a flannel and a towel. No prizes for guessing what is going on here – we are talking about foot-washing, the subject of today's reading. Do we have a volunteer to have their feet washed? *(It is up to you how much you make of this and how many feet you wash. If children are present I would do quite a lot as it is so visual and will strike them as pleasantly odd.)*

Did you know that in St John's Gospel there is no direct account of the beginning of Holy Communion – Jesus sharing the bread and wine with his friends? The Last Supper is there but no Holy Communion. It is in the other three Gospels and in Paul's First Letter to the Corinthians, but not St John. So if the only Gospel to survive had been St John I wonder if we would have had Holy Communion at all? Perhaps, instead we would have had this, foot-washing, which is in St John's account of the Last Supper but not in the other three Gospels.

Can you imagine it? Outside the church would be a sign which said 'Sunday at 10.00am – Holy Foot-Washing' and instead of coming forward to receive bread and wine people would remove their shoes and socks and queue up to have their feet washed? Yes – I think I prefer the bread and wine arrangement too, but it might make us think.

I don't suppose that foot-washing is going to catch on, but it ought not to be forgotten either. St John sets it at the very beginning of the Last Supper, and Jesus washes his disciples' feet. Remember that he washed the feet of Judas Iscariot too, as he was still there. And he had trouble with Peter who didn't want Jesus to lower himself by washing his, Peter's, feet. Jesus was the leader, the boss, the top man. They don't do the menial duties. Not usually in the world, says Jesus, but you are going to be different. I have washed your feet and you are to wash each other's feet.

That is it, really. Foot-washing was not a particularly nice duty in a hot dry country where feet would be dusty and smelly. Jesus did it for his disciples and that meant that there was no duty which was to be 'beneath them'. Nothing is too ordinary or menial for a Christian to do for others, because it wasn't for Jesus. Nothing and nobody is beneath us, however important we think we are.

It is important to come to church, to read the Bible and most of all to know Jesus. Once you do know Jesus you need to realise that he calls us to lives of service, to looking after each other, and that is not always fun or interesting. Sometimes it is dull, boring – and really not very nice.

Jesus told us to love one another – and he showed us that it can involve almost anything, even washing smelly old feet!

April Baptism

THE CRICKET BAT

Prop A cricket bat.

(This is personal to me because my father did take me to cricket and teach me to love it. It could apply to one's mother, an uncle, or an older brother/ sister – and it could be cricket or football, theatre or opera. The principle works with any of these variations. It is set out below as I would do it.)

Message As a demonstration of our love for them we must make the effort to bring children to faith.

Talk What have I got here? It is a cricket bat. The season is about to begin and I L-O-V-E cricket. That is nearly all down to my father. He took me to my first County Cricket match when I was not quite nine and the following year he bought me a membership. He sat with me while I chattered away when he would rather have been concentrating on the cricket. He tried to show me what makes a great player, rather than a good one. Most of all he let me learn through his love for the game. He took time and trouble. He did it because I was his son and he loved me and wanted me to share in one of the things he really cared about. He also took me to Stratford upon Avon to see Shakespeare performed excellently when I was much the same age.

Taking me did not enhance his experience of the cricket, or the theatre. On a purely practical level he would have enjoyed it much more without me. Indeed, I must have driven him mad with my cheerfully ignorant enthusiasm at times. But I am so grateful to him for it, and I hope I have given a little of the same to my children, and they will to theirs.

Primarily, he did it out of love. We want our children to know and enjoy the experiences that we have found valuable, and satisfying, and enriching. Whatever they are. Most really worthwhile things require time and trouble before a child really starts to understand for him- or herself. It is part of being a parent that you try and help your children discover for themselves the things that will make their lives more complete.

Today we have a Baptism. Children who are being baptised do not know what is going on. They will find it hard to discover faith, or come to a knowledge of God in Jesus, unless someone takes time and trouble to help them. It will not just happen.

My father was not alone in needing patience with me at the cricket. His best friend was often with us and he too had to put up with me at the cricket and he too did, and did it with good grace. And friends need to help with a child's faith development too and none more so than the god-parents.

My father took me to cricket, and to the theatre. He did something else too that I treasure. He took me to church. He showed me through his example that it was important. And because of that, though I had many years away from the church, it was always there and I was able, one day, to come back.

Cricket matters hugely to me (*wave cricket bat at congregation*) but God matters more that anything else. Help these children to know it for them-selves.

THE SCROLL

Prop A scroll, wrapped in a ribbon. *(I would use the Gospel reading for the day and type it up, unless you have someone in the church who can do fine italic writing and is prepared to do it for you.)*

Message All Christians have a duty to make sure the gospel is 'passed on'.

Talk What have I got here? It is a scroll and it contains the reading for today. I am going to pass it to *x* here at the front (yes, you can open it and look at it) and I want you to pass it on to the person next to you and for it to be passed round the congregation. Please look at it and then pass it on.

There is a small reason and a big reason for doing this. The small reason is as a reminder that when Jesus was visible on earth that was the way the readings were kept – in a scroll, even if rather larger than this one. The reader would be given the scroll and it would be unwound at the point the reading was to begin – not in a book form as today. The scroll would be, of course, if you think about it, of the Old Testament – we sometimes forget the Old Testament was the whole of Scripture for Jesus.

The big reason is in what I have asked you to do. To read it and pass it on. Christianity has always been spread that way. It has not always been in writing as most of the early Christians were 'converted' by hearing someone speak who could tell of what they had seen and heard or what someone they knew had seen and heard. After a while these people began to die and the Gospels were written down so the word could still be passed on. The gospel was spread by an existing Christian, or Christians, telling other people what they knew about Jesus AND by them showing the difference it made to their lives.

And how will Christianity be passed on to further generations? In exactly the same way. It will be delivered by Christian people who tell others about it, or bring them to church where they can hear about it, or offer them a Bible where they can read about it, or, ideally in a mixture of all of these ways. It's very similar to the way the first Christians went about it. It still requires the knowledge of God's love in Jesus to be handed on to others who have not heard it, or not fully received it. And it still requires those who do it to show by their lives that it makes a difference.

Sometimes people seem to think that this is the job of the clergy alone. It is their job, but not only their job. It is also the task of every Christian to seize the opportunities they have to spread the word and show what it means to them.

Hear the good news about Jesus. Pass it on.

THE TEAPOT

(containing real tea)

Prop A teapot (or a thermos flask) containing real tea. A cup (and milk and sugar should you wish).

Message Real Christian love is more than something nice.

Talk Do you know something? I would love a cup of tea. So it is a good thing I brought this along, a *pot/thermos* of tea. Yes, it is real tea. What would you love?

The trouble is that, well, it's the word 'love' that is the trouble. We would love a cup of tea, or to go to the cinema. Popular songs are all about love but it seems a very frothy, uncertain thing. 'Love' is used as an alternative for 'like', 'enjoy' or prefer'. It has reached the stage where if you don't say 'love' about something you are assumed to be indifferent or to actively dislike it. The word 'love' has become almost meaningless.

This makes it hard for those who are trying to sum up Christian faith to help others follow Jesus. We want to use a summary of the Great Commandment such as 'Love God, and love your neighbour as yourself' but we want it to mean something. We are afraid that if we say this those listening to us will translate it as 'Believe in God, and be nice to people', and that is nothing like enough.

Loving God is not about putting a tick in the right box on the census when you are asked for your religion. It is about believing passionately that God is the source of everything worthwhile in our world and our lives, and through that belief wanting to be as close to God as we can, and to feel God in our lives. It is about God actually coming before anything else in our lives, however worthwhile, even work, hobbies, families, friends. However hard it may be, we need to recognise God as first in our lives.

Loving our neighbour, *as ourselves*, is not about being nice to people, provided it does not interfere in our lives too much. It is about recognising that others are as much children of God as we are and deserve as good a life as possible. It includes doing to others as you would have them do to you, but it is much more than that. It is about offering concern and love to others regardless of whether they return it. Probably the finest description of it ever given is in Chapter 13 of St Paul's First Letter to the Corinthians. It involves effort, and is so much more than being nice.

It is not true. I wouldn't love a cup of tea, but I would quite like one. *(I pour out the tea – and then drink it!)*

Love is what Christians are asked to return to God and to show each other. It is a little word but it has a huge meaning. It is at the heart of the gospel of Jesus. Love God and love one another. And I do mean LOVE.

CARPENTRY TOOLS

Bible Reading: Mark 6:1-6; Matthew 13:53-58

Prop One or more carpentry tools (hammer, chisel, saw, etc).

Message Jesus was human, like us, so he can help humans, like us.

Talk What have I got here? Tools, or more specifically, carpentry tools. I bring them because the Gospels suggest, and tradition insists, that Joseph was a carpenter, and Mark says that Jesus was a carpenter too. Jesus is reckoned to be have been around 30 when he began his ministry, so he must have done something until then and it's hardly surprising that he followed the trade of his earthly father, Joseph.

I like to think of Jesus doing something both useful and creative – it seems rather appropriate. More than that though, it reminds us that Jesus was a human being like us. The Christmas story is important because it reminds us of this fact. Jesus was human, he didn't arrive fully formed as if from outer space. He was born to a human mother, Mary, and had to grow up and learn about being human. He grew up in a real village, in a real family, and he had to have a real job.

Jesus was fully human and that is very important. The Incarnation is the theological doctrine that Jesus was both human and divine, not some parts of one and some parts of the other – a kind of crossbreed – but both entirely human and entirely divine. That means that he belongs in the world of God and the world of us on earth, and by belonging to both he can help bring the two together. Jesus, because he was one of us, human, knows what it is like to be one of us with the ordinary challenges and problems, joys and possibilities of everyday life. He can help people like us because he is 'people like us' (forgive the grammar).

When you read the Gospels you hear many stories of ordinary life. Jesus told parables about a dangerous road, about a son who lets his father down, about sowing seeds and building things, about trade and work. He told these stories so that his hearers would recognise their world and see that God was to be found in it. He could tell the stories because it was a world he had known and a life he had lived.

Jesus the carpenter, who lived on earth as one of us, can help us and be with us. Jesus the carpenter – and my Lord.

W – H – Y ?

Prop A card (or three) with the letters W – H – Y

Message God's love for us is without limit.

Talk *(I would recruit a volunteer, or three, to hold up the cards when given the word to do so.)*

What are the three questions that parents most fear from their children (oh all right, other than THAT one)?

In third place, star of so many journeys, 'Are we nearly there yet ?'

In second place, 'Can I have *x* because all my friends have got one?'

In gold medal position, known and feared by parents in every culture and language. Please hold it up and show them for me:

W – H – Y?

Why? We who have been parents have all been there. Why? And you answer. Why? And again. Until finally, in desperation, you say something really reasonable like, 'Because I say so. OK?'

If you have been there you will know what I mean. There is something so constant, so unyielding about a small child in a 'Why' mood. And yet most parents cope with it pretty well, until they crack, and they usually feel bad about their outburst almost as soon as they have given way to it. Why? Oh no – I've done it, now. Why? Because we love our children and want them to learn and flourish.

Jesus once said that if we, bad as we can be, can still know how to be kind and generous to our children, how much more will God always be ready to be there for us. It is so obvious really and yet we can find it hard to believe. Why should God love us and look after us when we are not really much good or very important? For the same reason we love our children even when they drive us to distraction. Because we love them.

It's great news that God loves us too. Teach these children that God loves them, all the time, even when they are not acting in a very lovable way. God loves them and will never desert them. God is always there.

Why? There is only one answer.

God loves us. Thank God.

I'D NEVER NOTICED THAT!

Bible Reading: Luke 10:29-37 (The Good Samaritan)

Prop Something most people have not noticed.

(Very few people know everything about a church building. The visual aid is something most people will have seen many times and not noticed. Almost every church has one or more such things. For example, at my present church most people go to church walking over the monument to the man who was mainly responsible for having the church built. At another church where I served there was a monument in the churchyard to two people who were married for over 50 years in the early 1600s and married when neither of them was older than their mid-teens.)

Message Parables can show us something that was always there but we have never noticed before.

Talk What have I got here? Nothing, as it happens. I often show an object that I have concealed, but today is different. But I still have something to show you. Come with me. *(I then show them the tomb, the engraving, the pink giraffe – there really is one in the West Window at Worcester Cathedral – or whatever.)* Most of you will never have noticed it before. But now you have been shown it, you will always know about it, and be unable to miss it. There is a true story of a clergyman being shown the new lighting system that had just been installed at his church. The electrician asked him to turn the lights on and off to make sure they all worked. While he was doing this he suddenly saw a feature of the church he had never seen before. It had always been there, and he must have passed it dozens of times, but he had never noticed it. Until suddenly the lights were turned on and he could see it. Just like what happened to you today.

That is the way that parables work. They are great stories, but the really good thing about them is that you suddenly see things, often familiar things, in a way you had never done before. The lawyer knew the rules and he almost knew who his neighbour was, but was not quite sure. Jesus tells him this story about a dangerous bit of road everyone knew about, and when Jesus had finished the lawyer KNEW – his neighbour was his fellow man or woman in trouble. It is what I call the 'Now, I see!' moment and that is exactly what parables do. Once you 'see', it is just like the item in church you have never seen before – you will never forget that it is there.

We know the parable, of course. The expression 'a Good Samaritan' has passed into our language. Unfortunately we merely take it to mean helping someone out. That is only half true. The parable does not just tell us about someone who needed help, but that the person who helped him would have been regarded as an enemy. It was as if an Arab were to help a Jew in Jerusalem today, or a Catholic help a Protestant in some parts of Northern Ireland. Or, dare I admit it, a Christian help a Muslim in some parts of this country. It is not just the help that the story emphasises, but that the help comes from the one person from whom you would not expect it. It is the exact opposite of the saying, which I find quite un-Christian, 'Charity begins at home.'

Now I see! Do you? Then you will never be able to ignore it again.

THE NETTLE

Prop A nettle (or a weed – a nettle is better!).

Message You have to put effort in if you want a flourishing garden. Why should we assume that we can leave children to find out about faith without help from us?

Talk *(I am a hopeless gardener. As a result my garden nearly always has plenty of weeds and nettles despite the best efforts of my wife. If you are a keen and efficient gardener you will have to revise slightly, though there is bound to be a weed somewhere and the principle is unaltered.)*

What have I got here? It is fresh from my garden. Yes, it is a nettle. I am sorry to say that it wasn't too difficult to find because I am pretty useless in the garden. You may all be different and have beautiful and immaculate gardens, but if you are you will understand what I am about to tell you. It doesn't happen by accident, does it? My trouble in the garden is a mixture of lack of time, great ignorance and not actually enjoying gardening much. The result is this – my nettle.

Stay with the garden idea for a moment. Leave a garden for too long and it gets out of control. Take time and trouble and even I begin to see some results for the work put in. I have always liked the story of the vicar who leans over a fence and sees a gardener at work in a magnificent garden. The vicar says, 'Isn't it wonderful what God and man can do together in a garden?' And the gardener looks up, stretches their back and says, 'True, Vicar. But you should have seen the mess it was in when God had it on his own!'

You know that it is right in a garden. God has given gardens to us for us to look after – they are our responsibility. Why should it be any different with our children? In most ways I think we know that it is true for them as well. Our children will only become the flourishing people we want them to be if we take time and trouble helping them develop. Sometimes, though, we make an exception. We assume that our children will encounter God, find out about Jesus, and have a faith which will sustain them, without us doing anything to help. The school will do it, or the church, or the vicar!

Anyone but us. The truth is the same as with the nettle. Make the effort and you will see the results. Ignore it, and you cannot be surprised if the equivalent of spiritual weeds is all that can be found.

This applies most particularly to the parents and godparents – it's a responsibility you have taken on. It does affect every member of this church as well. We all have a duty to help and support whenever we get the opportunity. Jesus occasionally used the example of crops and harvest as a way of understanding how faith grows (the Parable of the Sower is one of the better known). It is up to us to make sure that the children baptised are nurtured in the faith so they grow and yield a harvest.

Remember my nettle. You have been warned!

THE HOBBY

Prop A crossword puzzle/a theatre ticket/a cricket bat.

(Whatever suits the person giving the address. They will know me as a cricket fanatic and in August this would be appropriate, but I am also a crossword enthusiast, and like going to the theatre. Someone else may play the trombone or do jigsaws.)

Message Some people think religion is a hobby for those who are that way inclined and have the time. It is not. Faith is about all of life and needs daily attention.

Talk What have I got here? And why? It is a crossword puzzle. Most days I have a go at the crossword in either *The Times* or the *Telegraph*. It is my lunch-time relaxation, but I also do the crossword when I am on holiday, so I suppose you could say it is a hobby of mine.

Now you might say, 'That's fascinating but what has it got to do with me, or with faith, which is presumably what the vicar (preacher, etc) is here to talk about?' While others might be thinking, 'Well, religion is a kind of hobby too, isn't it?' And that is the point I want to make.

Faith is **NOT** a hobby like cricket, or crosswords, or going to the theatre – all of which I enjoy very much. Faith is **NOT** an optional extra, tacked on to life by those who have the time, and who like 'that sort of thing'. Faith is about, and should affect, the whole of life, every part of it, every day. I don't mean that you spend all day in church or talking to God, though an occasional moment for prayer is always helpful. I mean that the sort of person you are, and how you live out daily life, is shaped and directed by what you really believe, in your innermost being. If you have a faith it will make the difference; the real faith you have and not just what you say you believe. What you are and what you do says far more about your faith than any number of words you can say.

Christians are those whose lives are shaped and directed by their experience of Jesus of Nazareth, encountered in the Bible, in the church and through their own experience. Christians want to live the sort of life Jesus guides them towards. They will not always succeed, but Christians will want to keep trying because they have come to accept that the life Jesus leads us towards is the only life really worth living.

And that is so much more than just a hobby. You could truthfully say that it is everything.

August Baptism

THE FOOTBALL SCARF

Prop A football scarf *(or a rugby scarf or a cricket hat – or some obvious symbol of support for a sporting team).*

Message Families often support a particular *football/cricket/rugby* team. They are quite literally a *Manchester United/Bristol City/Sheffield Wednesday* family. It should be the same with bringing up children. You should see yourselves as a 'Christian' family – and the children should know it as much as they know the team that you support.

Talk What have I got here? It is a football scarf. For, of course, *x* Football Club. If you wear this scarf no one is in any doubt which team is 'yours'.

I knew this family. *(This is absolutely true. I did, but there are many such families around. You may well be able to say this as truthfully, but if not you can always say, 'I heard of this family' – which you did, from me!)* Mum and Dad were supporters of Aston Villa. Actually that isn't true. They were not supporters. No, they were fanatics, and it ruled their lives in the football season. When I knew them they had two grown-up daughters, both in their early twenties. Both were also entirely committed to the cause of Aston Villa. Then one daughter married and produced the first grandchild, a little girl. I left their village when this girl was between three and four years old. That child had already been to Villa Park, had her own scarf – and I believe was able to enquire of the referee where he had left his glasses when giving a decision against her side!

That family knew 'what sort of family' they were – they were an Aston Villa family. There are lots of families just like them. The good news for me was that they were a 'Church of England' family too. Mum came to church regularly. Dad now and again. Both daughters were to be seen from time to time and the granddaughter was baptised and was being brought up in the Christian faith. Christian, as well as an Aston Villa supporter. And that was what made that family different. Lots of families, as I said, support a particular football team. Many fewer are the families who also know that they are a Christian family.

That is a real shame. It is important for children to know 'the sort of family you are'. I guess that most families have a variant on the saying 'We live by our rules, not other people's' (almost the only real answer you can give sometimes to the cry, 'But Jenny's family do it!'). It is a way of establishing your own attitudes and boundaries. It is important for children to know what their family are like. It is also important for children to know from their parents, and the godparents, that they belong to a Christian family, that this belief mattered to their parents so much that they had them baptised in church. 'We are that sort of family.'

Tell *the child/these children* being baptised today that they belong to a family, and that family can be identified by the way it looks at the world and the sort of things it finds important. It may involve support for a particular football team. Most important of all, it means they belong to a Christian family. Later in life *this child/these children* will decide for themselves which faith to follow, or to follow none, but remember, what you do now will help shape their decision.

For now, let them know what sort of family you are – a Christian family. Ensure that you show it to them in what you tell them and by how you live.

THE HAM SANDWICH

Bible Reading: Mark 7:14-23, or Acts 10:9-16 and following
(though it can be used without a specific reading)

Prop A ham sandwich (a real one – which will be eaten).

Message Don't get too bothered about the details, and the externals. It is what you are that really matters.

Talk What have I got here? Yes – it is a sandwich. Actually, it is a ham sandwich, and very good I am sure it will be. In fact, it looks so good that I think I am going to try it. *(With which the speaker takes a real bite and eats some of the sandwich.)* Yes, I was right, it is very good. Now if I was Jewish I would not have done that because they do not eat the product of a pig. Muslims also have strict rules about food, rules about what you can eat and how it is prepared. However, it is no part of my purpose to criticise other religions and their food rules, but these rules are not a part of Christianity.

Christianity has worried about food over the years. The early church had problems over Agape meals (a bit like a bring-and-share meal that some churches hold). They would not eat food that had been sacrificed in honour of pagan gods. At one time fasting was a part of much religious life (rather less so these days, I think). And to this day there are those who feel that, as a matter of belief, they must be vegetarian. However, from very early on the Christian Church has rarely worried about the particular food that is being offered or eaten, but has concentrated on what is really important.

So in Mark's Gospel, Jesus is reported as saying that 'nothing that enters a man from the outside can make him "unclean"' (Mark 7:18), and, 'What comes out of a man is what makes him "unclean"' (7:20). Or in Acts, Peter has a dream about being offered food to eat which he regards as unclean, only to be told 'Do not call anything impure that God has made clean' (Acts 10:15). Food matters but it is not what is most important. If by eating or not eating certain foods you show your devotion to God then that's good – but it is better to show your devotion by living the kind of life Jesus demonstrated. We are to follow Jesus' example and seek to live the life he modelled for us.

It is easy to mistake the detail for the substance. We have all met people who had a very strict code of conduct, and yet were hard and cold. Rules can help, but they must never get in the way of doing what is right. The test, as Jesus pointed out, is what a person is like and how they behave. And that is what really matters to God.

It is a very good ham sandwich (*takes another bite).*

THE CERTIFICATE

Prop One or more certificates *(in my case a Certificate of Theology, a Marriage Certificate or I could use my Chartered Accountant certificate. Others might use GCSEs or 'A' levels, or even a Life-saving Certificate).* Also the Baptism Card for the day.

Message Certificates recognise an important point in your life, and many then entitle you to live in a certain way, but they require you to keep working, learning and looking forward. They are often the beginning and not the end.

Talk What have I got here? Certificates, that's what. I must have received lots over the years. These two are my 'Certificate in Theology' and my 'Marriage Certificate' but I could have brought others. A certificate recognises an achievement in the past – an exam passed, a qualification completed or a certain musical standard obtained. The Marriage Certificate recognises that something important HAS happened.

So certificates are about the past, but they are nearly always about the future as well. An award at one level for music or swimming enables you to go on to another level. My Certificate of Theology was the forerunner to my ordination. The Marriage Certificate is clearly about life after the ceremony, not before it.

Certificates recognise what has happened but they are nearly always about what will happen as well. I remember that when I qualified as an accountant I burned all my old study papers, but I very quickly I discovered that I was going to have to carry on learning and working at learning if I wanted to do the job well. And when I passed my Driving Test I realised almost at once that this was where the real learning began.

And this brings me to this other certificate. It is a Baptism Card. It marks the fact that later in this service *this child/these children* will be baptised. Something will happen, and once it has happened it cannot un-happen (if you will forgive the somewhat tortuous grammar). And yet, the truth about Baptism is that it is really the beginning and not the end. It starts you off as a member of the church family. No one can take the certificate away from you, no one can 'un-baptise' you. But a real Christian finds out very quickly that, as with most other certificates, it may entitle you to do or be part of something, but if you are going to do it properly you will have to carry on working, learning, and looking forward.

Keep this card. Then, when the time is right, show it to *him/her/them* and explain that it marks not the end of the story but the beginning – and help them find their way.

October Family Service

THE INSURANCE POLICY

Bible Reading: Mathew 6:25-34

Prop A life insurance policy.

Message Trusting God does not mean not using our common sense.

Talk What have I got here? It is an insurance policy. One of mine. It pays out a benefit in the event of something happening in the future. Most of us have got one or more of them. It is one of the things that you do to look after yourself and the family. But then in the Gospel reading today we hear the following words (verse 34) 'Therefore, do not worry about tomorrow'. So am I being unfaithful to the gospel?

There are Christians who would take this verse literally. There are people who have lived this way, and some still do. There are members of Christian churches who always want their church to spend any surplus or give it away, and not save for future bills. However, the majority of Christians do not live this way. They do make provision for the future. They make plans. They do so because of other sayings of Jesus, such as one in Luke's Gospel (Chapter 14). In this passage Jesus points out that a man who is going to build a tower needs to make sure he has enough money to finish it, or a king going to war has to check that he has enough troops in his army.

So do we ignore what Jesus seems to say today, 'Therefore, do not worry about tomorrow'? Surprisingly, in view of my insurance policy, I say NO. While I cannot follow those who take this verse literally I am impressed by the fact that many Christians I have known who 'take no thought for the morrow' (as the Authorised Version put it) do manage quite well and so often they do seem to lead a charmed life – or perhaps it is blessed. They do not panic about the future or spend their time worrying about it. They get on with what needs doing in God's world now.

I have also observed that parishes which spend all their time fretting about money, and who hardly ever give anything away because they 'need every penny we can get', do not flourish as well as those who demonstrate a generosity of heart and spirit, even when they need money themselves.

The lesson is not, I conclude, that it is wrong to make plans or prepare properly. The mistake is to let the problems get you down. God is with us whatever befalls us. God does provide what we need. So we can and must trust God. It is sensible to make plans to ensure we do the things that need doing – providing we do it trusting God, in a spirit of service and generosity to others as well as for ourselves.

Even to the extent of taking out insurance. Provided we don't put our faith in that and our money, rather than God.

BAPTISM SYMBOLS
(CROSS, WATER, CANDLE)

Prop A cross, water (in a bottle, perhaps) and a Baptism candle.

Message Remember the signs of Baptism afterwards.

Talk *(I cannot imagine anyone who is doing the talk at a Baptism, especially if they are administering the Baptism afterwards, will be unable to say something about the symbols present at a Baptism. It is included with these talks because I have found it helpful to use them as the 'trigger' for the talk now and again. Each minister will have their own interpretation so I simply offer mine as a guide, especially in so far as I keep to one point per symbol.)*

I usually begin a talk at a Baptism with, 'What have I got here?' Then I show one, or more, objects that I hope will stick in the mind of the congregation because they are so unusual. Today is different. I have three objects – but they are not in the least unusual for a Baptism, in fact they are fundamental to it. The three objects are a cross, some water, and a candle. All three will be used at the Baptism: the sign of the cross made on the forehead of each child to be baptised; the water, the element at Baptism that everyone knows about; and the candle which we give to each family at the end of the service.

I begin with the cross. I think we always should begin with the cross. We are so used to it that we can forget what it is all about. The cross at Baptism reminds us that all that we do is derived from, and goes back to, the man on the cross, a good man dying because of all the evil that there is in the world. Christianity goes back to a man the world would have regarded as a complete failure, a convicted criminal, and it reminds us that God's ways are often very different from our ways.

Water is the most basic material on earth. It is the source of all growth, and without it there is nothing. We use it at Baptism because we believe Jesus to have been baptised by John the Baptist, and in being baptised Jesus linked himself to all of us in the most ordinary part of life. Nothing is too ordinary for Jesus and he can be with us in the most down to earth parts of life, if we will let him.

The candle represents Jesus as the Light of the world. He is an example for all of us to follow, and in giving a candle to each person we baptise, we give them a symbol by which they can remember the Light of Jesus. BUT, and this is important, Christians are called to be Jesus' light to others. Others should be able to look at a Christian and see something of the way of Jesus in them.

Three things which are an essential part of this service: the cross, the water and the candle. May they remind all of us here today that God's way is not the world's way, that God in Jesus is with us in the most ordinary part of life, and that we, having Jesus in our lives, must show him to others.

May we know it for ourselves and teach it to *this child/these children*.

November Family Service

THE CREDIT CARD (OFFER)

Prop A credit card offer received through the post, or in a newspaper. Alternatively, if one of those is not available, a credit card.

Message Jesus gives it to you straight.

Talk What have I got here? It is an offer for a new credit card. Actually, I already have a credit card, or two. I try to use them sensibly and, used that way, they are very handy. Like most things it is how you use them that matters.

But this offers me so much. All that extra money I could use and for almost no cost. Things I would really like which I cannot afford – a nice holiday perhaps, or some furniture, or one of those enormous televisions. All on this card and it will cost me almost nothing! It sounds too good to be true, doesn't it?

Well, it is!! I hope you know it is not really like that. The rate of interest might be low for a while but I still have to pay the money back or pay interest at a rate far more than most other sources of money. If I can't afford that holiday, I still can't. Shame really.

It is all a bit of a con. It looks very nice, but it is an illusion. And it is so easy to fall for it because we want to believe what they say. We want to believe that we can have it all, at no real cost. But it's not true.

Everything has a cost to it. Jesus repeatedly made this clear. He told people that following him was not an easy option, and that it might even lead to pain or trouble. It was NOT guaranteed to give you a nice life with everything you wanted. It may not result in success or popularity. Jesus' offer is almost the exact opposite of most credit card offers. Jesus tells us that we should live the way he showed us, the way God wants us to. We should do it because it is right and the way of God, and be prepared to accept the consequences. It cost Jesus the ultimate price – his life – and throughout the centuries other followers have been prepared to pay the same price.

It may not cost us like that, but it might. We have been warned. At least through the Bible we know what we are getting. Be under no illusions, unlike with this wretched offer, and you will find that Jesus' way is the most worthwhile – as long as you understand the terms.

(Tear up offer as a finale.)

November Baptism

THE INSTRUCTION BOOK

Prop An instruction book (video recorder, DVD, digital camera).

Message Faith can be made too complicated but in essence it is quite simple.

Talk What have I got here? It is the instruction book for my *video recorder/DVD/digital camera*. Look at it – page upon page of detailed and complicated instructions. Perhaps it makes sense in the original Japanese or Korean – but somehow I doubt it.

I can remember my first video recorder. It was a large machine – you needed two people to lift it, but it was incredibly simple. You could either record or playback, fast-forward or rewind. Four buttons – easy. There was a clock as well and I could use that too. My last video recorder had so many functions I was amazed it couldn't cook dinner. It had buttons everywhere – but actually all I wanted was to record, playback, fast-forward or rewind.

My digital camera is worse. It is very small, but you need to go on a course before you can use it. All I want to do is take photographs that I can print from my computer and send on the Internet, but I think the instructions for that must be contained in volume 2!

I am not quite as bad with technology as I may be making out, but that is not the point. The point is that what I want from these pieces of equipment is really very simple, and so I think it is for most of us. Somehow, the makers have made it so complicated and it need not be so. All that is needed is for the first part of the book to tell you how to do all the things everyone wants and for the last part to enable you to do the more imaginative and clever bits. They have made it far too complicated.

I think the church, which includes me as one of its ministers, can make faith too complicated when in essence it is really quite simple. Believe in God who is the source of everything. Follow Jesus who is the best view of God in a human being we are ever going to have. Know that the Holy Spirit wasn't just at work while Jesus was on earth – he's still at work today. That's not the whole of faith, but it is a very good place to start.

Believe in God, live as Jesus taught, and let the Spirit encourage and sustain you. Learn this for yourselves and teach this to *the child/children* being baptised today.

It doesn't have to be complicated.

THE FEATHER DUSTER

Prop A feather duster.

Message It is good to get ourselves ready for Christmas.

Talk What have I got here? Yes – it's a feather duster. When my mother comes to visit we give the house a bit of a clean – not that it's dirty the rest of the time – but we make an extra effort for a visitor. She is important to us and we want to make her welcome.

If the Queen, or the Mayor, or the Archbishop, or even the boss (depending on your lifestyle and taste) were coming to dinner, you would make an effort, wouldn't you? The best plates, the shiniest glasses and the best wine would all come out of the cupboards. I know that's what we would do.

At Christmas we remember when Jesus came to earth, but sometimes we can become so busy we forget all about him. Often, we are too busy with Christmas to have time for Christ. There is, I know, a lot to be done and, like all of you I have cards to write, presents to buy and a tree to decorate. I am sure though that you can see my point – somehow, it's all too easy to leave Jesus out.

I want us to make as much effort getting ourselves ready for Jesus as we do preparing our houses for visitors. There is no more important person ever going to visit us than Jesus. We need to apply the feather duster to ourselves!

I want us all to do three things.

Firstly, I want us all to stop for a few minutes each day and remember that Christmas has to begin with Jesus.

Secondly, I ask you to read one of the Gospels right through during Advent. Take Mark – there are only 16 chapters and the birth of the baby is never even mentioned – so a chapter a day should do it. Remind yourself what happened to the baby of Bethlehem; the man he became; what he did and taught; and how he was crucified and raised from death.

Finally, I hope you will reach Christmas resolved to follow the man the baby became and to live the way he taught and showed, loving God and loving your neighbour.

Then you and your house will both be ready for Christmas visitors.

Take a feather duster to both.

THE TEDDY BEAR

Prop A teddy bear, or other soft toy (ideally belonging to the person giving the talk).

Message Jesus was a real human baby, just like any one of us.

Talk What have I got here? It is a teddy bear. My teddy bear. He is as old as me, given to me at my first Christmas. He is old and battered (possibly just like me!), but he is very special and I would not trade him for anything.

Has anyone else here got a teddy bear, or similar soft toy? Who has? *(I would probably go around the congregation finding out about their bears. I wouldn't just ask the children, I would also ask the adults as most adults have a teddy bear at home somewhere.)* What a lot of bears and other toys! It is hard to imagine a modern child in this country without a bear or something similar.

Jesus would not have had a teddy bear – because they had not been invented back then. They belong to the last two hundred years – long after the birth of Jesus. But, and this is the important bit, Jesus would have had toys to play with, the same sort of toys that all the other children around him had to play with, and with Joseph being a carpenter I expect he had some very nice wooden toys.

This matters because some people don't really think of Jesus as human. There are those who like the Christmas story and enjoy hearing about the birth of the baby, but who do not link it to the man the baby grew up to become and what he said and did. Then there are others, who like the man Jesus and what he said and did, but because they rightly call him the Son of God, they do not understand that he was a real human baby, just like any one of us. He was not beamed down from heaven, like Superman from Planet Krypton. He was one of us. He began life as a baby dependent on the people around him, most of all his mother, and grew up as all of us do.

This is indeed good news. If Jesus was born, and grew, and lived as we all have to – and we know that he had to die, as we all must – then he knows what it is like to be human. He can help us in times of trouble, and support us when life is hard. He can also show us how to live, through what he said and did, because when he said and did these things he was showing us how to fulfil our potential as humans.

The *child/children* being baptised today *is/are* too young to know what is going on. They are being baptised into the group of people, called the church, who look to Jesus of Nazareth, as both our best human view of God, and as the best way to be human. They need to be taught that Jesus was special, that he was the Son of God, but that he was, entirely and unmistakably, human.

And, if he had been born today, I am sure he would have a teddy bear – almost as nice as mine.